Table of Contents

Chapter 1: Executive Summary...3

Chapter 2: Introduction...4

  Why Strategy is Required in Starting a Business..5

    Traditional Business Plan...6

Chapter 3: High Level Issues Affecting the Start Up of Businesses.....................7

Identify and exploiting the right opportunity..10

Literature Vs Industry...12

Chapter 4: Research into Causes of Failed Entrepreneurial Ventures.................16

Failed Start Up Businesses..22

Further Research: A Local Failed Start Up Business Experience.......................24

Chapter 5: How Strategy Is Missing..26

Chapter 6: The Importance of Strategy..29

Five Forces Model...29

Chapter 7: Strategic Business Planning..33

Strategic Road Map...33

Pathway to Successful Strategy Execution...35

Chapter 8: Change Management & Resilience...38

Lack of Requisite Skills and Training..38

Differentiation Strategy...40

Licensing or Certification for Start-Up Entrepreneurs....................................44

Chapter9: Referencing..46

Dedication

I dedicate this book to the late **Reverend Rose Akua Ampofo**. Thanks for coming to my rescue when the situation was hopeless. May the Lord keep your soul in perfect peace.

To My Wife & Kids

Thanks for believing in me and being there for me through thick and thin. I wouldn't be here without you. I love you unconditionally

Chapter 1

Executive Summary

Are entrepreneurs born or made? Some may argue that entrepreneurs are born but there is the school of thought that believe that entrepreneurs are made. it is widely believed that one out of two businesses fail within the first four years. Subsequently, there is a research to ascertain the actual rate of failure and what has been contributing to the high rate failure of start-up businesses.

The research confirms that at least fifty percent of businesses are unable to survive beyond the fifth year of existence. This is very worrying and so the research delves deeper to find out why most start-up businesses are failing. Are business owners equipped to meet the expectations of the business and shareholders? Do they have a plan of execution at all?

A plan of execution involves the strategic steps to achieve the set milestones within a business plan. The plan of execution shows how the entrepreneur can meet the set targets of the business, but this is dependent on the strengths of the management team and to a certain extent, the lifestyle and commitment of the entrepreneur.

The study shows how the high-street banks and Community Development Financial Institutions (CDFI) are advancing loans to these start-up enterprises on the cheap without the proper review of the business plans and the ability to deliver as normally stated in the business plan.

The research concludes that if nothing is done to enforce the execution of strategic plans to deliver the set objectives of a business, then there is highly likelihood of small businesses no longer able to generate the revenues needed by the economy.

To enforce this strategic plan, one must know what it entails. The study shows that any strategic plan should involve Porter's five forces including the following

- The threat of new entrants
- The threat of substitute products
- The bargaining power of buyers
- The bargaining power of suppliers
- The intensity of rivalry among competitors

The analysis of the above shall serve as the basis to set targets and hire resources for the successful delivery of the business plan. As part of strategy, resilience must be built in the business plan as well. Most start-up entrepreneurs are not equipped for both success and failure. In other words, they are so passionate and optimistic about the business idea but fail to recognise the obstacles and changes in the real world.

There must not be just the strategic execution of plan but also the equipping of entrepreneurs to be resilient and resolute in their pursuit of success. This research thus recommends the licensing and training of start-up entrepreneurs to minimise the rate of business failure and double the revenue being made by the sector within the next decade.

Chapter 2: Introduction

Small and Start Up businesses rely heavily on finance from the traditional banks and venture capitalists. According to a story carried out by 'The Telegraph', more than 600,000 new businesses were expected to be launched in 2015 (The Telegraph, 14th May 2016) in the UK and 581, 000 new businesses were set up in 2014. The report revealed that the annual start rates have increased from 440,600 in 2011 to a ground breaking 581,173 in 2014. The government is at the centre of championing the cause for business start-ups through various initiatives including Start Up Britain.

Although the banks have tightened their lending to start-up businesses, it has become relatively easy to access loans to start a business. The government continue to fund start-up businesses through the Start Up loan scheme (source: 2010-2015 Government Policy for Business Enterprise Report)

Theo Paphitis, the British successful serial entrepreneur has recently called for entrepreneurship to be included in the national curriculum due to 50% of start-up businesses failing in the first couple of years (theguardian.com). According to Theo Paphitis, most of these businesses fail because the entrepreneurs are not doing their 'homework' before starting the businesses. Failing to plan is planning to fail.

Why Strategy is required in starting a business

Vision is nothing without execution. Whenever anyone asks me about vision, I get very nervous. You have got to be able to tie it back to strategy, you have got to tie accountability to things (Mark Hurd, Chief Executive, Hewlett Packard)

A traditional business plan has the following:

- Background of the business
- Description of business
- Mission Statement
- Marketing Research
- SWOT Analysis
- Financial projection/funds required
- Competitors
- Management Team
- Marketing Strategy/Plan
- Exit Strategy

The above topics forms a general business plan being used by a lot of business owners or entrepreneurs. In my opinion, this plan is missing a strategy to execute the business plan to perfection

Every company or business must have its vision and strategy to execute. For instance, British Airways vision is to be the world's favourite airline and to achieve that, British Airways marketing drive is to put customers first, supported by internal training and employee communication and revamping the corporate image. General Electric's vision is to be first or second in all chosen markets and the strategy is 'if a business is not first or second in its market, close it, sell or fix it. Emphasise ownership, teamwork and enterprise in everything. Become a "boundary less" organisation, shifting resources and expertise to wherever they are most needed' (Michel Syrett, Successful Strategy Execution)

The traditional business plan being produced by a lot of entrepreneurs lacks the strategy to implement the business plan. A marketing strategy is not the vehicle or mode to get the business to achieve its vision. Hence an entrepreneur must detail the activities and the resources responsible to carry out the strategy. An entrepreneur must own the vision and produce a plan in the form of a project plan that includes timelines for delivery of the milestones identified in the business plan. This will be the strategy to implement the plan and to achieve its outcomes.

Strategy is perceived as more than an intended outcome based on a top down procedure and as a more complex, emergent, bottom up process developed throughout the organisation with the participation of multiple organisational members (Sotirios et al, Strategy Practice)

Business strategy is never a once and for all event- it goes on and on. There is the need to continually review strategic objectives because the environment is always changing. Depending on the stance that a company adopts, the purpose of strategy is either to make a business 'fit' into its environment or to use the resources of the business to 'change the rules of the game'. By achieving this, the probability that the business will survive and prosper are enhanced (David Campbell et al, Introduction to Business Strategy pp 1).

Chapter 3

High Level Issues affecting the start-up of businesses and their survival

Figure1: Start-up businesses in the UK from 2012-2015 (Case Study)

According to the published report in February 2015 on Small Firms 2010-2015 by the Prime Minister's Advisor on Enterprise, there are 5.2 million number of small firms, an increase of 760,000 since 2010. The business population increased by 330,000 within a year

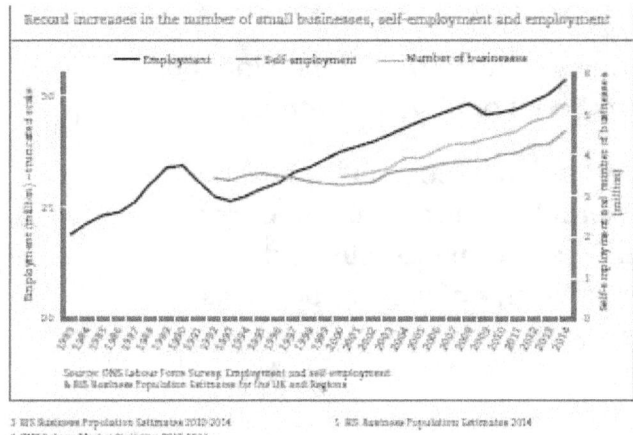

Source: The Report on Small Firms (2010-2015)

According to the report, UK is one of the best places in the world to run a business and entrepreneurial spirit is on the increase amongst the young people aged 18-24. The UK was rated in the top 10 in the world for doing business.

Organisations like 'Start Up Britain' are lending to small businesses in the UK and so it is no surprise that the number of start-ups have sharply increased over the years. We have seen TV programmes, 'Dragon Den' and 'The Apprentice' becoming very popular within the last decade hence giving the rise in business start-ups. However, although these TV programmes are good in promoting enterprise among the young, they have failed to show the reality of starting and running businesses in the real world. This has misled a lot of who have no skills in management or how to start and run a business venturing into business as an opportunity rather than a career.

Although the government efforts must be commended, the alarming rate of loans being given to start-up businesses should be a major cause of concern. According to the report on Small firms published by the government, £131 million has already been given by the government to start up 25,000 businesses across the country since 2012. The report however failed to state the number of start-up businesses that have failed since 2012.

According to a report authored by Elizabeth Anderson and published in the Telegraph in October 2014, more than half of the UK new businesses don't survive beyond five years. The survival rates are lower than before the financial crisis in 2008 (Half of UK Start Up fail within 5 years, Elizabeth Anderson)

"The UK is a wonderful place to start business, but survival rates are low. The recession has had an unsteadying effect on small businesses. Once these businesses are up and running, owners are also struggling to plan for the long term"

According to the report, 61 percent of 160 owners surveyed said they lacked the confidence in their ability to achieve 3 years' consecutive growth.

This report resonates with me because I started a business in 2005 but the business failed in 2011. I started the business with high hopes and secured loans from the high-street banks. There was no mentorship or support provided by the bank as advertised by the bank. As an entrepreneur, I was eager and passionate to do well and so worked very hard to get some clients signing up for the business services.

However, although the business was generating revenue, it was not enough to cover for the overheads. The business had to continue paying for the premises, had to pay contractors and employees and then the financial crisis which started in 2008 began to have its toll on the growth of the business.

As an entrepreneur, the only way out of this crisis was to try to diversify to gain access to new markets.

The company diversified and offered new services, however, that did not improve the financial state of the business as more money had to be paid out to the business creditors. Subsequently, the business had to fold up as it was no longer solvent.

The business had to compete with the big businesses for the same contracts and opportunities. It was extremely difficult for the business to compete because these big businesses had the resources and the financial ability to out manoeuvre any small firm. To win any viable contract, one must prove that the business has the financial record to be able to deliver and often the requirements are too much for a small business to compete. The banks and the government are not actually warning entrepreneurs about this unequal playing field for both small and big businesses.

Another killer of small businesses is the bank's demand for loan repayments even in times of difficulty. The banks will chase for repayments irrespective of the circumstances and the state that the business find itself in. No breaks are given, and the business must struggle to make the repayments on time inclusive of rents, taxes, PAYEs and any other regular bills.

The very sad thing is the banks and other creditors are likely to take the very businesses or entrepreneurs that they willingly lent funds to court. I had fallen a victim and, so it amazes me how governments still look on unconcerned while the banks continue to give loans to start-up businesses without warning them of the risks involved.

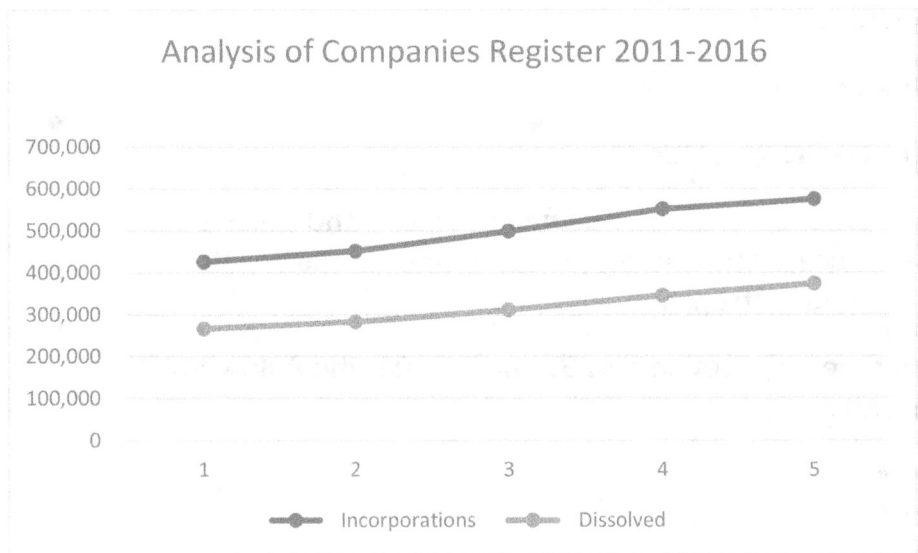

(Source: UK Companies House 2016)

According to the above data compiled by Companies House in the UK, the average age of a company still trading is 8.4 years. However, the average age of companies going bust or closing is 5.4 years. Since 2011, we have had about 2.5m businesses incorporated but 1.5m of these businesses have closed within the same period. This represents about 60% of businesses closing by the fifth year of existence and only 40% surviving beyond the 5th year. This percentage is staggering and therefore calls for the investigation as to why businesses are failing at such a high rate.

Just as my experience in starting up my business in 2005, a lot of these businesses that folded were unable to get out of debts and some of these entrepreneurs chose to bury their heads in the sand as they could not do anything about the situation. Many have not shown leadership and I believe leadership is in entrenched in strategy.

"Bill George in his book Seven lessons of leading in a crisis argues that there are several lesson leaders should learn from the latest recession

- Face Reality- which starts with those in charge acknowledging their role in creating the problems that must be solved. Widespread recognition of reality, even if painful, is crucial before problems can be solved. Myopia suffocates organisations ability to respond to emerging threats and opportunities.
- No matter how bad things are, they will get worse. Faced with bad news, many leaders cannot believe that things are so grim, and they try to convince the bearers of bad news of this. They think that swift action will make the problems go away and underestimate the work needed. It is far better for leaders to anticipate the worst" (Jeremy Kourdi, Business Strategy pp148)

Literature on Entrepreneurship & Strategy

Identifying and exploiting the right opportunity

An entrepreneur is a person who organises a business venture and takes on the financial risk to initiate, operate and manage their business (Martin Ofori-Atta, how to become a successful entrepreneur)

According to the criteria outlined by Steven and Spence (2008) the following must be taken into consideration

- Realness of opportunity
- Durability of opportunity
- Marshalling the resources
- Managing the venture
- Harvesting the venture

Business Feasibility Factors:

- Realness of opportunity: The entrepreneur has got to answer some tough questions. First, they must prove that the business idea can stand the test of time. The questions to be answered are outlined below:
  1. Is this a real business?
  2. Are customers identifiable and reachable?
  3. Does the product/service deliver superior value?
  4. Is the economic model viable? Is the profit potential adequate?
  5. Does it open options?
- Durability of Opportunity: The opportunity must be a durable one. In other words, it should not be one that last for just sometime but must be in demand from one generation to the other. The following

questions must be answered by the entrepreneur in relation to the durability:

1. Will the opportunity enable the business to develop distinctive competencies?
2. Can the business build entry barriers?
3. Can the entrepreneur identify and address stakeholder goals and needs?
4. Is the business ready to respond to change (external and internal)?

- **Marshalling the Resources:** The entrepreneur must be able to gather the resources required to deliver the objectives of the business venture.
    1. Can the entrepreneur identify and access critical resources?
    2. Can the entrepreneur be able to monitor and manage critical resources?
- **Managing and Harvesting the Venture:** The entrepreneur must be equipped to manage and set the parameters or benchmarks to exit the business. In other words, the business must have an exit strategy.
    1. Are there realistic mechanisms for exiting the business venture?
    2. Can any investor understand the conditions to trigger the sale of the business or shares?

Finally, and importantly whoever you are also matters. It cannot be ruled out the fit between person and type of process is equally important. It may be necessary for individuals to use the approach they prefer and make that work regardless of what the situation 'objectively' calls for (Sara Carter et al, Enterprise and Small business pp 117)

Using the Stevenson & Spence criteria conduct (2008), a personal feasibility analysis must also be carried out

- **Entrepreneur Personal Goals:** The entrepreneur must ask whether the venture is consistent with their personal goals and values. Are they comfortable with the personal risk/reward profile of the business? They must be prepared to take the financial risk involved to set up and run the business
- **Entrepreneur Capabilities:** The entrepreneur must define a useful role specific to his/her capabilities. Does the entrepreneur have the skills and experience required to add value to the business venture?
- **The Entrepreneur's Lifestyle:** The entrepreneur must be able to accept the impact of the venture on their lifestyle. This could impact on their personal finances and so a plan must be in place to manage the personal finances

- The Entrepreneur must also understand the potential impact this will have on their personal relationships. There must be the evidence of engagement of spouses or partners to show their commitment to the vision.

Literature Vs Industry

The traditional business plan being used in the real world has got a lot of these key academic steps missing. In the real world, one need just a business plan to apply for business loans and it has become so easy to get a business loan of up to £25,000 in the UK.

The typical business plan adopted in the real world has the following topics:

- Executive Summary
- General Company Description
- Products and Services
- Marketing Plan
- Operational Plan
- Management and Organisation
- Start-up Expenses and Capitalisation
- Financial Plan

Executive Summary: The entrepreneur gives a brief description of the product or service and who their targeted customers are. This section entails the goals of the business and the main competition. The entrepreneur uses this section to state how much money he/she want if applying for a loan and how this money will help the business idea to become profitable.

General Company Description: In this section, the entrepreneur includes the mission statement, company goals and objectives, philosophy of your business, a description of the type of ownership the company entails, the industry and strengths of the company.

Products and Services: The entrepreneur uses this section to describe the products and services. The opportunity is given to prove the uniqueness of the product or service. The advantage of product or service over its competitors

Marketing Plan

This is the integral part of the entrepreneur's plan as the venture will only succeed with effective marketing plan. This is based on the research that he or she carries out. The research gathered must be the basis of the sales forecast. The research consists of published information sources such as magazine, newspaper, journal and industry content

Operational Plan

In this section, the entrepreneur is supposed to explain the daily operation plan of the business, its location, equipment, people, processes and environment. This includes the following:

- Production
- Location
- Personnel
- Inventory
- Suppliers
- Credit Policies
- Managing accounts receivables
- Managing accounts payable

Management & Organisation

The entrepreneur uses this section to introduce the management team and their background, experience, core competencies, key positions and their functions.

Personal Financial Statement

The entrepreneur can attach all the necessary personal financial statements and for all other stakeholders. This section can be used to list all assets and liabilities separate from the business and net personal worth.

Start Up Expenses and Capitalisation

This section can be used by the entrepreneur to estimate the start-up costs including the operating expenses and the working capital. The entrepreneur can include sources for information, loan amounts and terms, and how much investment is required and the percentage of ownership.

Financial Plan

The financial plan must consist of a 12-month profit and loss projection, a four-year profit and loss projection, a cash flow forecast, a forecasted balance sheet and a break even financial calculation, which offer financial estimates for the future of the business.

- 12-month profit and loss accounts
- Four – Year Profit Forecast
- Projected Cash flow
- Balance Sheet
- Break-Even Analysis

(Source: Martin Ofori-Atta, How to Become a Successful Entrepreneur pp 33-45)

Although the above topics within the business plan are very important, I believe the key ingredients that will certainly make the business successful are missing. These are:

- Realness of the opportunity
- Durability of the opportunity
- Marshalling the resources
- Managing the venture
- Harvesting the venture
  (source: Exploring Business Opportunities Slides, WBS Entrepreneurship module)

Although some of the topics within the business plan are meant to get the answers to some of these issues, the traditional business plan still lacks the credibility to carry the in-depth analysis to prove the viability of any business proposal.

For instance, the realness of the opportunity cannot simply be based on the marketing research and plan. Although there may be a gap on the market for the product or service being offered, the product or service might not be in demand as forecasted. The reason being that a service or a product might not be on the market at a moment in time for a reason.

This gives credence to the fact that a small business introduction of a service or product might not gain the required response compared to one that is introduced by worldwide known player or brand. Hence further options need to be explored by the small business before launching a product or service. These options should include the formation of partnerships with some of these big brands or companies. Of course, there is the risk of rejection and perhaps the theft of innovative ideas but small businesses must always use 'Non-Disclosure Agreements' as part of the approach in engaging these big firms.

A small business may have a very brilliant idea but the realness of that opportunity has got to be assessed against these benchmarks, whether the service or product can withstand the test of time and can gain the confidence of the public as proven in this case.

The durability of the business cannot just be measured by the mere financial projection and operational plan. It must be holistically reviewed against the entrepreneur's

- Personal goals: judge whether the venture is consistent with their goals and values. Is it the best option now for moving toward those goals?
    - Is the entrepreneur comfortable with the personal risks or reward profile of the business?
    - Does the core team have the capabilities to deliver? This is dependent on the capability of the entrepreneur to raise a competent team to deliver the set objectives of the business plan.
    - The lifestyle of the entrepreneur must be assessed as part of the business plan. The entrepreneur must understand the impact of the business on their lifestyle

The key individual must have sufficient commitment to the start-up. In support of this notion, Baum and Locke (2004) demonstrated the importance of passion and tenacity for the long-term success of the new venture (Sarah Carter et al, Enterprise and Small Business pp97)

Unfortunately, this is missing in the traditional business plan and no wonder many businesses are failing. Loans are being advanced to many entrepreneurs who lacks the passion and the commitment to succeed during adversity.

Chapter 4: Research into Causes of Failed Entrepreneurial Ventures

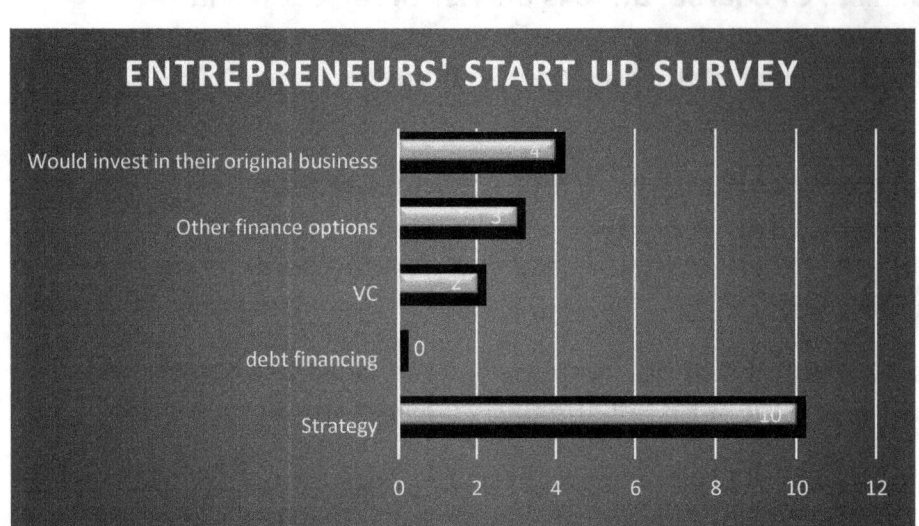

A survey was conducted using ten MBA students with the intention to start up their own business. The questions used as part of the survey are as follows:

- Prior to the MBA Entrepreneurial Module, would you have invested in your business plan?
- Would you consider other sources of finances for your business following the MBA Course?
- Would you consider debt financing following the MBA Entrepreneurial module?
- Would you include strategy as part of the business plan following the module?

The first question took the wind out of their sails and only four answered that they would have invested in their own business prior to the MBA Entrepreneurial module. This is after gaining an insight into the real -world operation of a business. Hence one need to take stock before deciding on the right source of finance to go for. The reason why there was only four who were still confident to invest in their own business is because the rest realised that doing business takes more than a title but real commitment and the passion to make the business a successful one. Further reasons could be attributed to the lack of robust business plan and the need for the entrepreneur to own the risks and outcomes right from the onset.

The answers to the second and third questions were interesting and shall serve as a reminder to many entrepreneurs to 'count their chickens before they are hatched'. Prior to attending the MBA module, majority of these start-up entrepreneurs would have opted for debt financing but after gaining insight into the operation of real-world business, all of them declined to even consider debt financing as an option

They realised that short term loan is not the answer as it puts a lot of pressure on the business and eventually cripple the business because of the elevated risk of failing to meet expectations. Whether the business is doing well or not, the bank expects repayments to be made on time every month. This study shows that these start-up entrepreneurs are now aware of the real risk of getting a start -up loan to finance their respective ventures.

They would rather seek other sources of funding such as Venture Capitalist investment. Venture Capital is more suited to start-up businesses because of the following reasons:

- Tailored to meet the needs of small companies and start-ups
- No bank debts
- Venture managers often used to be successful entrepreneurs themselves

Venture Capital :Tailored to meet the needs of small companies and start-ups

Venture Capital investment is ideal for start-ups because Venture capitalists are always looking for a business idea that could generate high revenue and hence would give them high return of investment.

"Once you have proved that the idea can work by means of prototype, an economic study, a marketing analysis, or some other means, you are able to have a good shot at obtaining financing from the venture capital community. The company must be one or two years away from cash flow break-even. As a result, the venture capital company will want a considerable return on its investment for taking an elevated risk" (David Gladstone et al, Venture Capital Handbook pp21)

The Trap of Loans

If the business secures a venture capitalist investment, the entrepreneur need not to worry about monthly repayments. Thus, giving the entrepreneur to start the venture successfully without the undue pressure of making repayments within the first few years. Unfortunately, many entrepreneurs have been caught in the web of financial debts and are unable to get the business to a healthy state. Subsequently, the business becomes insolvent and liquidated. The Venture Capitalist on the other hand is always looking to exit when the business is making huge profits and therefore shares the risk with the entrepreneur. In the event of business failure, the venture capitalist takes nothing from the business and the entrepreneur does not have to repay as it is not a loan.

Venture Managers

Venture managers often used to be successful entrepreneurs themselves and so are prepared to support the entrepreneurs to meet targets and for the venture to become a successful one. The VC want to see the business grow as fast as possible in order to maximise profits. The VC wants to see sales go up and want profits as these are the basic objectives for being an investor. The VC wants to see that the entrepreneur builds a strong management team to guarantee success. If the company grows rapidly and becomes large, the VC would be looking toward liquidity. Venture capitalists are not in the business of owning and operating businesses. They are in the business of investing for a period, helping build up a business and then cashing in on those investments by selling their positions (David Gladstone et al, Venture Capital Handbook pp 309-310)

Armed with this information, the selected would be entrepreneurs are now cautious and are more determined to become successful entrepreneurs. Hence their judgement is now influenced by the above factors and willing to consider even other options of financing which does not include debt

From the above table, it is evidently clear that all the start-up entrepreneurs would include strategy in the development of their business plan. It is interesting as some entrepreneurs would want many to believe that they have strategy as part of their plans but obviously, this so-called strategy is missing in the implementation of their business plans.

Companies can be successful only if they manage to align their strategy and organisation with the environment they operate in. As the environment is constantly changing, this means that enduring success depends on a company's ability constantly to adapt its strategy and organisation (Christian Stadler, Enduring Success pp 41)

Strategy must be aligned to both the organisation and environment they operate in to ensure success. Strategy is dynamic and not static; hence entrepreneur always need to update the strategy to meet the needs of their organisation and environment. Lessons have been learnt from the big companies.

The international strategies of the French cement producers Lafarge and Ciments Francais affirm that companies need to find strategies that prepare them for a changing environment. In the 1970s the two firms were about the same size, but they chose radically different growth strategies. Lafarge pursued a strategy of internationalisation, while Ciments Francais focused on France. When the oil crisis slowed demand for cement in France, Lafarge was active in 15 international markets, while Ciment Francais had only minor operations in Morocco. The former could offset losses. The latter could not (Christian Stadler, Enduring Success pp 41)

It is no wonder that these entrepreneurs take strategy very seriously following the lessons learnt from attending the MBA course. They are of the conclusion that a successful business plan must be based on the entrepreneur's strategic roadmap.

Section A - ANALYSIS OF THE COMPANIES[1] REGISTER
Table A2: Summary of Changes in the Number of Private Companies on The Register 2011-12 to 2015-16

PRIVATE COMPANIES	2011-12	2012-13	2013-14	2014-15	2015-16
UNITED KINGDOM					
Incorporations	455,008	482,357	532,533	585,242	610,966
Dissolved	286,798	301,885	331,527	368,954	399,237

In liquidation/course of removal	245,777	265,168	281,119	259,496	244,161
Effective number on register at end of period	2,605,075	2,771,368	2,961,386	3,197,128	3,427,555
Of which: Unlimited	6,024	4,790	4,712	4,611	4,488
Private companies as percentage of United Kingdom effective register	99.7%	99.7%	99.8%	99.8%	99.8%

(Source: Companies House 2016)

A research was done to analyse the data of all incorporated private companies within the last five years against the private companies that have been dissolved within the same period.

From the data taken from companies' house in the United Kingdom, a total of 2.7m businesses were incorporated between 2011 and 2016. Within the same period, a total of 1.7m businesses were dissolved. It is evidently clear that a staggering 50% of the businesses became insolvent and was dissolved. It is no wonder that many researchers have confirmed that 50% of start-up businesses are not able to survive beyond 5 years

There is surely underlying reason as to why 50% of businesses are not able to survive beyond 5 years

Further Research:

An interview with Neil Hutchinson who graduated from Warwick Business School in 2000 and now owns a number of successful companies.

He first won award for a website he designed about reggae music and this helped him to get a job in web designing.

"I started to learn about internet marketing back in 2002 and soon realised that he was a better at working out how to drive traffic to a site"

He started to work make money from internet marketing whilst designing websites. He soon quit his job and concentrated fully in becoming a full-time traffic broker in 2004.

His quest to start his own business was not stopped by his poor credit rating. "My fund-raising options were quite limited, I had a bad credit rating from my time at University" admits Hutchinson

He approached a former employer and managed to persuade him to lend a six-figure sum at zero percent equity. His former employer agreed to lend him the money but he would take fifty percent of the profits until he could pay him back.

"Within a year he had mad all his money back, he had more than doubled his investment. " Having a profitable business model from the early days meant Hutchinson didn't need to raise finance and wasn't accountable to anyone but himself. This gave him the flexibility to expand beyond internet marketing into different areas of the internet. He confirmed this in his own words,

"I think that was pivotal to expanding into a portfolio of businesses rather than only having one and focussing on one thing."   (Advice from an Internet Entrepreneur, Warwick Business School)

From the experience of Neil Hutchinson, one can say that he used a strategy which was dependent on his skills and passion. It wasn't anything to do with producing a business plan and financial statements. Literally, his former employer lent him the money he wanted not because of their relationship but the fact that the employer had the confidence in him because of the knowledge of his skills and passion.

Neil used his unique skills set to start the business without even relying on the traditional banks and venture capitalists. This should not be treated as a 'one off' but a clear model that can be used to start and grow businesses. Neil has proven that with the right strategy coupled with the skills set and the right lifestyle, one can only succeed.

Some might argue that without the borrowed funds from his former employer, he wouldn't have made it as a successful entrepreneur. The funds actually helped him but because he had the right strategy and attitude, he excelled and now has multiple firms. Others failed miserably even though they got loans and the investments

Failed Start Up Businesses

Zirtual provided on-demand virtual assistants. Instead of taking the gig economy model and using only contract workers, Zirtual differentiated itself by having full-time employees. Each assistant would work multiple accounts, depending on the workload, making it cheaper for corporate clients.

Why it closed: In August, Zirtual **laid off its 400 employees in the night** via an e-mail, after a last-minute Hail Mary round of funding failed to come through. CEO Maren Kate Donovan later said the "numbers were f-----" and the company had over-staffed without having matching demand.

Looking back, **she told Fortune** that she should have hired a full-time CFO and had a proper board for the company. Zirtual's assets were acquired in October by Fundable.

Money raised: $5.5 million, including from Jason Calacanis, Mayfield Fund, Tony Hsieh, and the VegasTechFund.

(Source: http://uk.businessinsider.com/startups-that-failed-in-2015-2015-12?r=US&IR=T/#homejoy-2)

Analysis: Although this start-up company raised $5.5m, it was unable to survive because of the lack of a robust strategy. First, the CEO should have had the foresight to hire contractors to meet the demand of signed contract. It should not have been based on just assumptions and forecasts, but a business model fit for purpose. One will wonder how the company was able to raise $5.5m because one could have a wonderful idea but then investors need to probe the mode of delivery. Based on experience, I believe that this mistake could have been avoided if the CEO was interrogated on how the business would deliver and meet its targets. The plan of employing full time virtual assistants irrespective of the number of existing contracts could have been interrogated to seek its long-term viability.

2nd Case Study (Failed Start Up Business)

What was it: Secret was an app that allowed for anonymous posting of snippets of text, often rumours or confessions, that were shared with people.

It was huge at SXSW and rose along with other anonymous apps like Whisper and Yik Yak. But like many anonymous apps, Secret had problems with cyberbullying and eventually redesigned itself to look like competitor Yik Yak.

Why it closed: In his farewell blog, CEO David Byttow wrote that Secret "does not represent the vision I had when starting the company." He continued: "I believe in honest, open communication and creative expression, and anonymity is a great device to achieve it. But it's also the ultimate double-edged sword, which must be wielded with great respect and care."

Money raised: $35 million. Byttow noted that most of the money would be returned to investors.

(Source: http://uk.businessinsider.com/startups-that-failed-in-2015-2015-12?r=US&IR=T/#homejoy-2)

Analysis

This failure was mainly caused by a lack of vision. Vision must encompass strategy and so vision without strategy is nothing but a dream. It is obvious that the CEO did not believe in the business he started. Where was the conviction? Whose idea was it? If the idea was David's, why the sudden turn around? This indicates that the entrepreneur lacked the conviction and the belief in his own business idea. This is why the lifestyle of the entrepreneur needs to be considered as part of starting up a successful business. In this case, the entrepreneur failed to analyse the risks involved and putting in place the necessary counter measures to mitigate such risk from happening. Conviction of an idea would lead to proper analysis and any risks identified before the start of the business.

3rd **Case Study (Failed Business Start Up)**

What was it: The music-streaming service launched in 2006 as a site where users could upload their music for others to listen to it. It immediately ran into legal problems over concerns about copyright violations, and over the years tried to sign contracts with one of the largest royalty companies. That company said it never really received information from Grooveshark on what was being streamed, so it — and pretty much every other major music company — started suing them.

Why it closed: In its goodbye notes, published as part of its settlement conference, the streaming site acknowledged that "despite the best of intentions," it made mistakes by failing to secure licenses from rights holders for the vast amount of music on the service.

Money raised: $6 million.

Analysis: This failure was caused by lack of foresight and the need to assess the competition and the legal requirements within the industry. One cannot just start a business without researching on both the legal and commercial requirements to make the business successful. This is just incompetence on the part of the entrepreneur and his team.

Further Research: A Local Failed Start Up Business Experience

A company that specialised in Customer Relationship Management Software and computer software related training started trading in 2007. Within just 12 months of operating as a business, the company could secure loans from banks. Although the business had secured clients and needed the funds to meet the targets, there was no robust strategy to implement the business plan.

The banks merely extended the loan to this company based on the business plan and bank statements. Although the entrepreneur had one on one interview with the bank officials, they never queried the credibility of the business plan because according to the director/entrepreneur, they (banks) were satisfied with the financial forecast.

After just 14 months, the business started struggling due to the Global financial crisis. Most of the business clients started to struggle as well and collapsed. The company did not have the strategy in place to deal with such economic downturn. Subsequently, the business could not keep up with its loans repayments and eventually the director was taken to court by the CDFI. Although the company was a registered limited company, the director was taken to court and his personal assets were nearly confiscated. The director had to represent himself at the county court as he could not afford the solicitors fees. The case dragged on in the court for 12 months as the CDFI was bent on the confiscation of the director's personal assets.

Eventually, the court passed judgement in favour of the director for a percentage of the debt to be paid. The order was passed for both parties to reach an agreement on how that percentage would be paid. This case was an exception as most directors or entrepreneurs' personal assets have been repossessed due to their businesses failing.

Perhaps the business would have still been trading if there was a robust strategy in place to deliver the objectives of the company. Therefore, banks must also be held accountable for their decision to lend to start-up businesses. If they know what they are doing, then they must be able to identify the risks and not just base their decision on financial statements presented by the entrepreneurs. The balancing of future accounts based on a three to five-year account cannot be the yardstick to assessing the robustness of a business plan. Hence, if they lend to these business, they must accept the risk of losing the funds and should be held responsible as well and not just the owner(s) of the business.

If the business had the strategy to diversify to other untapped market, perhaps it would have still been trading. At that time, there was the emerging economies that were not affected by the credit crunch. These included India, South Africa, Brazil, China and Russia known as the BRICS. These countries were thriving even when the credit crunch was at its worst and that was the time for technology companies in the UK to reach out to customers in these countries. However, this depended on the strategy of the business and not the sales forecast within a business plan.

This may be controversial to the reader but there is a clear distinction between the traditional business plan and strategy as proven in this research so far. The research has so proven that businesses continue to write their business plan around the following topics

1. Marketing Research and plan
2. Operations
3. Competitors
4. Management team
5. Products and Services
6. Financials
7. SWOT Analysis

There are some who may argue that the SWOT (Strengths, Weaknesses, Opportunities and Threats) analysis deals with risks of the business, hence it gives the fair assessment of the business. This study shall disapprove this misconception.

Chapter 5: How strategy is missing

From the above, it is evidently clear that most entrepreneurs would not consider debts financing as the main source of funding their start -up businesses. This is subject to entrepreneurs being educated about the high risk that debt financing pose to start-up businesses.

It is interesting that these entrepreneurs after attending an MBA entrepreneurship module suddenly are more cautious in choosing the source of funding for their start-up businesses. However, this information is not out there for every entrepreneur to be able to make the decision based on the holistic review of the information available. Majority of these entrepreneurs who took part in this survey are now more conscious of the relevance of strategy to their business venture.

It is evidently clear that the entrepreneurs of these failed businesses discussed above would do things differently if given the second chance. There is one common missing in their business start-up and that is a real robust strategy to deliver the goal and objectives of the business.

Strategies can only be sustained by clarity of purpose and clarity of purpose can only be achieved through changes in behaviour. The capacity for people to get the wrong end of the stick is never ending and constantly reinforced by poor management. Persistent but sensitive vigilance is needed to check false perception and over interpretation of simple objectives (Michael Syrett, Successful Strategy Execution pp 25)

Clarity of purpose can only be achieved through changes in behaviour. In setting the objectives of the business, one must know that the set objectives can only be achieved based on a pragmatic strategy. This must take into consideration changes due to external factors.

Many entrepreneurs prepare their business plans without taking into consideration the risk of failing or encountering crisis. Face reality- which starts with those in charge acknowledging their role in creating problems that must be solved. Widespread recognition of reality, even if painful, is crucial before problems can be solved. Myopia suffocates organisations ability to respond to emerging threats and opportunities. As Jamie Dimon, chief executive of JP Morgan Chase, comments: it's not sufficient to have one person on your team who is a truth teller. Everyone on the team must be candid in sharing the entire truth no matter how painful it is. How can we solve problems, if we don't acknowledge they exist? (Jeremy Kourdi, Business Strategy pp 148)

A lot of entrepreneurs are failing to recognise that failure is part of success. Hence, they need to build a business which is prepared to fail but won't let that deter them from making a success out of the 'failed attempt'.

Rita Gunther McGrath is a professor at Columbia Business School and focuses on strategy and innovation in today's challenging environment for business. Her research has looked at the mechanisms for competitions and how organisation fail. From 2010, her team identified companies with a market capitalisation of more than $1billion and identified those that had been able to grow revenue by 5% for each of the previous five years. During that period, the growth in GDP was around 4% and so these companies were outperforming the national economy in terms of their growth.

The team found only 8 percent of companies were above 5 percent growth threshold and a repeat of the work for the period from 2000 to 2004 was similarly disappointing, highlighting only 15 percent of firms.

Finally, the team homed in on the companies that had been able to achieve that 5 percent revenue growth year in, year out over the ten-year period to 2009. The work then considered the three main competitors for each of these special ten companies and compared them to one another. A key finding was that these companies had long term perspectives on where they wanted to get to but more importantly, they recognised that what they are doing today will not deliver future growth. They were saying that no matter how good their advantages in the market today, that's not going to be enough for the future (Richard Jones, Strategy Genius pp 89)

This finding is quite interesting as this confirm the reason why many start-up businesses are failing to survive beyond their fifth year of existence. It is because they have no strategic plan to meet the future requirements of the industry or the market they are operating in.

The environment around some companies has changed so radically that the idea of creating and maintaining a sustainable competitive advantage may be unattainable. Secondly, companies cannot afford to rest on whatever feat they have achieved today because the world will change around us and so they need to change with it.

For instance, prior to Skype launching their services, the telecom companies were charging customers high fees to make international calls. The telecom companies were making huge profits until Skype launched their services in 2003.

The telecom companies could charge what they wished in the absence of any real competitions, enabling them to make good profits on these calls. Skype was introduced in 2003 to make free calls between PCs, but the opportunity to make free calls from PCs and transfer the call around the world on the internet was quickly identified. These calls would only incur a small charge in the destination country where they leave the internet and essentially becomes a local call.

The result was the extraordinary growth in the use of Skype, with 24.7 per cent of global international calls being carried over by Skype in 2011. Skype's entry into the market has both taken away significant market share from the traditional telco players and driven down prices so far that customers are now paying just 1-2 per cent of the price they used to pay for international calls (source: Richard A D Jones, Strategy Genius pp 89-90)

The lesson drawn from this case study is that the telco companies failed to put in place the strategy that would have still safeguarded their number one place in the industry as far as international calls was concerned.

They were complacent because of their success but failed to strategize for the future. A company could be doing well at present but fails to recognise the need to plan to stay relevant. Strategy is about understanding where you are now, where you are heading and how you will get there.

Chapter 6: The Importance of Strategy

Five Forces Model

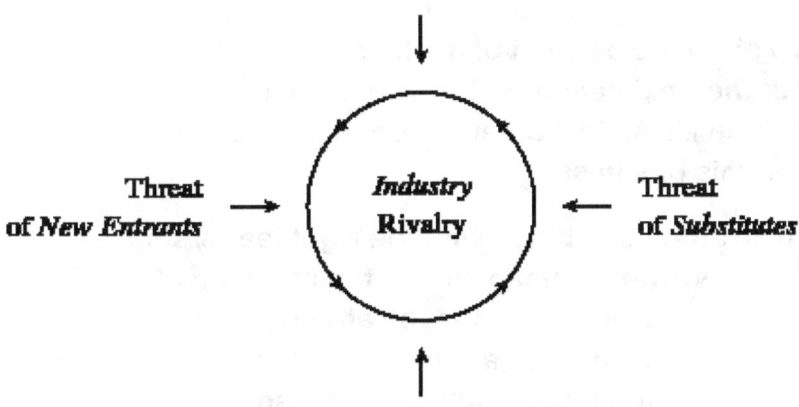

(Source: Wikipedia five forces Model)

The five forces model developed Michael Porter shows that a company is influenced by several factors including the actions of competitors in their chosen markets. The competitive rivalry with four other major influences - buyers, suppliers, potential entrants to into the market and the potential of substitution

Power of Buyers: This is the extent of power that buyers can have on the market regarding the price they pay, terms they will agree to, service agreements and specifications.

An entrepreneur looking to open a supermarket should be careful as the buyer's power on this pushes prices down and so failure to lower the prices could reduce the number of customers. They will go established supermarkets who are more interested in the volume of customers and will do anything to keep their customers happy.

Threat of substitutes:

The competition on the market has got to be assessed because a customer can easily opt for another product or service that is the same as the one on offer. The threat of a substitute if ignored can easily ruin a business venture.

Blockbuster DVD Rental business was doing so well until the emergence of Netflix and Amazon online video rental. Although it was obvious that Netflix and Amazon were on the heels of Blockbuster, they (Blockbuster) failed to recognise the threat that Netflix posed.

Entrepreneurs in starting up their business ventures must be aware of the ability for inexperienced players to credibly enter and disrupt the market. They must consider the barriers to entry or barriers that could be erected to prevent another company entering their market (Richard A D Jones, Strategy Genius pp 102-103)

This research clearly shows how about 50 percent of businesses are unable to survive beyond the fifth year of their existence. At the backdrop of this finding, we have found out how some MBA start-up entrepreneurs are now conscious of including strategy in this business.

They have realised that the right strategy combined with the right leadership or management of the business. The strategy encapsulates the ambition of the entrepreneur and how they are prepared to own that strategic plan until that plan is implemented. A lot of these businesses are not surviving beyond 5 years because they failed to put in a strategy that would have saved them from collapsing. The threat of substitutes has been ignored by many start-up entrepreneurs. The power of buyers and suppliers has also been ignored and this has not really been assessed by the high-street banks nor any other the lending and thus loans advanced to these businesses are mainly based on optimism.

Five forces should be a staple part of a strategic assessment. According to Richard a D Jones (author of Strategy Genius), far too often 'competitors' section of the business plan become a listing of the competitors or the competition. The content relating to the competition should be about what they are doing that is making life easier or harder for them. These may include new products, exclusive offers, improved terms, businesses leaving the market, businesses joining the market -everything that is impacting on the success of the business

The entrepreneur must own this analysis and then use that as the basis to set realistic targets. This will also enable the entrepreneur to have a robust plan not just for the interim but for the long-term success of the company. It will guide the entrepreneur in choosing the resources and the skills required to get there. However, many entrepreneurs are producing business plan based on their convictions to succeed instead of showing proof of the pragmatic plan to achieve the business objectives.

It is good to have the conviction to succeed but then this must be backed by the evidence on the ground to meet the targets. I believe strongly as the author of this research work that businesses that gets venture capitalist investment are more likely to succeed because proper due diligence is done using the above criteria to make decisions.

As previously discussed, a lot of the venture capitalists are successful entrepreneurs and, so they are ready to support the business to revise the business plan and focus on the right strategy to make the business venture a success.

Although some of the businesses that receives investments from venture capitalists fails, the percentage of failure is very small. Most Venture Capital investments are only offered subject to the following conditions:

- Criminal records check to ensure that the person is credible
- Lifestyle and profession of the entrepreneur(s) to ensure that their interests are aligned with the business objectives
- Credit Searches to ensure that the entrepreneur is free from any financial debts
- Holistic review of the business plan against any external forces
- Recommendation of credible strategic plan to guarantee success
- Some of the Investors can act as non-executive directors
- Targets reviewed to release any further funds

On the other hand, government agencies and even high street banks are lending substantial amount of money to start up entrepreneurs on the back of just one or two meetings and receipt of a business plan. If the 'numbers' stuck up, the loan will be advanced without any further reviews or getting the entrepreneur to prove how the targets or milestones shall be achieved.

No wonder, a lot of pressure are now exerted on the limited resources of the start-up businesses as majority must repay loans at the very initial stage of the business. Servicing loans at the initial stage of a business can be very daunting and stressful as all resources can be very stretched. Subsequently, if the business face issues or financial crisis, it is more likely to collapse within even the first thirty-six month of operation.

The lessons drawn from the case study of another entrepreneur is for start-up entrepreneurs to start in a very small way without loans if possible. The onus is on the entrepreneur to start building the business from the scratch with the limited resources available. From this entrepreneur's experience, loans cannot be relied upon to either engineer growth of the company or as a guarantee for successful start-up. Loans advanced to the start-up businesses are often not sufficient to even get the businesses to the stage of generating its own revenue. However, most entrepreneurs often are tempted to take these loans because they are so desperate to start the venture but some of them end up woefully failing.

Mum of four Sophie was handed £26,000 on a TV programme to start her dressmaking business but three months after being handed the funds, she is back on claiming benefits. Mum of four had wanted to provide a better future for her kids by setting up her own company. Lee, the programme's welfare expert advised her that the company would need the time for it to begin providing the sort of steady income she needs to live a comfortable life (thesun.co.uk, 21/03/17). The obvious question is whether the £26000 was enough for her to maintain her lifestyle and at the same time fund the successful start-up of the business until when the business could generate regular revenue? The business plan should be able to answer this question, however, when the CDFIs and the high-street banks are eager to lend the money just to meet targets and tick boxes while on the other hand, the entrepreneurs are desperate to take whatever is on offer to start the business without being fully aware of the consequences.

Good management must resist both the internal and external pressures to force new business into the old holes, simply because those holes already exist. Once a company allows structure to run its operation, it is only a few missed opportunities away from total stagnation (Marc McCormak, what they don't teach you at Harvard University pp 167)

Chapter 7

Strategic business planning

As discussed in the previous chapter, venture capitalist investments are subject to the following conditions

- Integrity of the entrepreneur
- Lifestyle and relevant experience in the chosen industry
- Credit worthiness of the entrepreneur
- Robust business plan
- Strategic road map to achieve the set objectives of the business
- Strong management team
- Tranches of funds release subject to performance

An entrepreneur must be able to prove beyond every reasonable doubt that he or she is more than capable to deliver. That does not mean an entrepreneur must be a 'magician' but one who has got the eyes and the character of an eagle. They can adapt quickly to terrible changing conditions and at the same time able to soar to dizzy heights.

The entrepreneur must be the first or a leader in their chosen market with the vision to do the following which are very consistent

- Produce significant return on capital
- Be Innovative and creative in their product development, service design and delivery and work practices
- Be ethical, socially aware and environmentally responsible in conducting their business

However, the entrepreneur must own the strategic road map to ensure that the vision becomes a reality.

The strategic road map may include the model advanced by Michel Syrett for successful execution of strategy as detailed below:

Focus:

- Review performance against targets regularly to ensure effective alignment of business units, teams and individuals to key strategic goals
- Foster a culture of Innovation to allow business units, teams and individuals the freedom

- Anticipate the likely change that will impact on the strategy and ensure that strategic goals are adjusted and updated

Freedom

- Create the right **focus** using cross functional theses to unite the whole organisation
- Break key goals into business unit, team and individual objectives to create **clarity** of role
- Support the introduction of these objectives with the right **communication** and consultation
- Identify the **behaviour** needed to fulfil these objectives and inculcate these using coaching and other personal support
- Introduce new **measurement** systems to provide the right milestones of achievement

(Michel Syrett, Successful Strategy Execution pp132)

Produce Significant Return on Capital

The entrepreneur must have the mindset to produce significant return on capital and to do that, he or she must set up the system to make this happen. Return of Investment is key to the success of the business because it urges the entrepreneur on to make the business profitable. No one sets up a business to make losses or to break even. The primary goal is to make the business profitable and thereby set the environment for investors to get the returns on their investments. A business that cannot be profitable must be shut down as it would be just waste of time and resources.

Innovative and creative in product development

Whatever the product or service is, the entrepreneur must have the creative awareness to adapt to the environment or the market to stay relevant always. The reason why most businesses fail is not just because of lack of funds but the lack of awareness to stay relevant to the market. As previously discussed, Blockbuster Video Rental was an American based provider of home movie and video game rental services with over 8000 stores. However, because of the failure to recognise the threat that its competitors posed, the company eventually went out of business and filed for bankruptcy in 2010 (source: en.wikipedia.org/wiki/blockbuster LLC)

They simply ignored the competition from Netflix and other online video on demand services and thus going bankrupt in 2010. The company should have been creative by recognising the demand for online video on demand service. The refusal to modify its services contributed to the sudden failure and bankruptcy. This should be a lesson for all start-up businesses.

According to Michel Syrett's pathway to successful strategy execution, there should be the focus to do the following as mentioned above:

1. REVIEW PERFORMANCE AGAINST TARGETS REGULARLY TO ENSURE THE EFFECTIVE ALLIGNMENT OF BUSINESS UNITS, TEAMS AND INDIVIDUALS TO KEY STRATEGIC GOALS

Every business plan must have key milestones to be achieved and the entrepreneur must have a review plan to assess performance against the targets. The set milestones should drive the entire workforce with the singleness of purpose to meet those targets. It is no good preparing the forecasted balance sheet and financial spreadsheet without a concrete plan in place to achieve the projected sales or figures.

2. FOSTER A CULTURE OF INNOVATION TO ALLOW BUSINESS UNITS, TEAMS TO FULFILL THEIR OBJECTIVES

Innovation is key for a business to stay relevant on the market despite the seasons. The seasons may affect the demand of a product and it may also impact on the trend of the industry. Innovation allows teams or businesses to modify the product or service being rendered to meet the current needs of their customers. Failure to stay innovative can negatively impact on the business as customers' needs may suddenly change due to the season

3. ANTICIPATE THE LIKELY CHANGE THAT WILL IMPACT ON THE BUSINESS AND ENSURE THAT THE STRATEGIC GOALS ARE UPDATED

The business must anticipate change in the business environment or change in the industry. This is linked to staying innovative as changes in the business world can affect business operations. Subsequently, the entrepreneur must raise a team that are ready and competent to manage changes effectively. Failure to manage change can lead to the collapse of the business venture.

In managing change, strategic goals must also be updated to reflect the change of the direction of the company. The leadership of the company must be prepared to take tough decisions to effectively manage the change

"Dealing with uncertainty should come down to this. Employees must respond quickly and creatively to the unexpected and devise counter moves and initiatives under crisis conditions. This means that people at all levels must relentlessly review existing projects and processes and discard those that have lost their relevance" (Michel Syrett, Successful Strategy Execution)

Management must face the reality and it starts with those in charge acknowledging their role in creating problems that must be solved. The widespread recognition of reality, even if painful, is crucial before problems can be solved. Myopia suffocates organisations' ability to respond to emerging threats and opportunities. Chief Executive of JP Morgan once said that it's not sufficient to have one person on the team who is a truth teller. Everyone on the team must be candid in sharing the entire truth, no matter how painful it is. No business can solve problems relating to changes or crisis if they don't acknowledge they exist. (Jeremy Kourdi, Business Strategy pp 148)

While these objectives are set, there must be the freedom within the organisation to create the culture that will get these objectives to be achieved. The following must be considered in creating the right culture within the business.

1. BREAK KEY GOALS INTO BUSINESS UNIT, TEAM AND INDIVIDUAL OBJECTIVES TO CREATE CLARITY OF ROLE

The culture within the business must allow goals to be broken down into phases and assign to the best team within the organisation. The best team to deliver each 'phase' of the project (goals) must be based on the capabilities of the members of each team. This will be the basis of defining responsibilities within a team and the emphasis shall be on the clarity of expectations

2. COMMUNICATION PLAN

There must be effective communication plan to report on the progress of each project within the organisation. The clarity on the expectations sets the mandate for each team to report to management based on the responsibilities and strengths. This allows the management to take quick decisions to deal with urgent issues.

3. BEHAVIOUR

The behaviour of the organisation is crucial for success. The vision of the organisation must shape the behaviour of the employees. This might need training and coaching of the teams within the business. The behaviour shapes the focus of the organisation to become very successful. Training equips the employees to learn what is required of them and how they must behave corporately to achieve their goals.

4. MEASUREMENT

Systems must be in place to measure the success or progress of each team delivering the objectives of the business. Measurement is key to keeping records of achievements and then compare to periods of decline or failure. This analysis will show the causes of the decline or failure as both periods are recorded and can easily be accessed via the system in place.

If an organisation benefits from the right focus but does not have the capacity to respond creatively, the execution of a strategy will be undermined by a lack of responsibility for it among the workforce, a lack of collaboration between essential work units or strategic partners and friction at middle or junior management levels. By contrast, if the business already has the right creative freedom but the direction provided by senior executives-in terms of overall strategy, stated goals and priorities, measures and milestones or the right pace is misplaced, its ability to respond will be undermined by a failure to see the bigger picture, uneven progress, little focus of energy and effort and poor resource allocation. It is only when effective leadership is supported by a change management capability throughout the organisation will it achieve focused performance, total commitment to a responsibility for the solution, and the necessary collaboration and ability to adapt. This produce the resilience to face and overcome an almost constant state of external uncertainty (Michel Syrett, Successful Strategy Execution pp133)

The focus and freedom factors as discussed above would create the conducive environment to produce significant return on their investment. The significant return on investment will enable the entrepreneur to successfully sell their stake of the business or take the business to the next level.

Chapter 8:

Change Management & Resilience

Lack of Requisite Skills and Training

The research carried out above shows how entrepreneurs are ill equipped to start and manage a business venture within this ever changing social and technological world. The survey conducted proves that most entrepreneurs would do things differently if they are trained and made aware of the 'real world' related risks

"Vision without execution is nothing. Whenever anyone asks me about vision, I get very nervous. You have got to be able to tie it back to strategy; you have got to tie accountability to things"- Mark Hurd (Chief Executive, Hewlett Packard)

It is good to have a business plan but is it enough to achieve the set objectives and for the business to thrive even in the absence of the founders? The vision is important but vision without an execution strategy has caused many businesses to fail.

The Centre for Economic and Business Research has predicted that small businesses in the UK will increase their total economic contribution to £217bn by 2020 (source: http://startups.co.uk/uk-small-businesses-contribute-217bn-economy-2020/)

Judging by the high rate of current business failure, the above target of £217bn might not be realised by 2020. This is like a bubble waiting to burst if this trend of start-up business model can stay the same. It will not be a surprise if the average business is unable to survive in its third year.

A lot of these start-up entrepreneurs lack the skills and experience to successfully run a business from the cradle to medium sized companies. The study carried out shows the result of randomly chosen MBA students whose opinion about how to start a business changed following the attendance of an entrepreneurial module.

The opinion changed because they gained the knowledge of running a successful business during any crisis and the influence of external factors and risks. The research further on showed three typical start-up businesses that failed despite raising the funds required. These start-up businesses lacked something in common and that is an effective strategy to implement a successful business idea. An interview with Neil Hutchinson proves that with right attitude coupled with a robust strategy, one can be successful no matter the hurdles and challenges that the business would come across.

It therefore behoves on the government to train start-up entrepreneurs in the following areas

- Leadership
- Strategy

This will get them ready to deal with any unforeseen circumstances and effectively deal with crisis as well. This will reduce the rate of business failure significantly and double the contribution that the sector provides to the economy.

According to Lara Morgan (author of More Balls than Most), the following rules must not be ignored when starting a business

- Change is the norm for a growing business. The entrepreneur and the team must embrace change to maximise their potential. The foundations must be set early as a bedrock of the culture
- Commitment comes from self-belief when the entrepreneur knows what is right for the business
- It is better to make hideous redundancy decisions and see them through fairly

The question is, are all entrepreneurs aware of these? That is a fair question but unfortunately most start-up entrepreneurs start their ventures without knowing the 'full picture'. In other words, they are unaware of the challenges in the real world and unfortunately the government is not doing much to tackle this issue.

The government must as a matter of urgency roll out the 'Silicon Valley' model of the US across the country. According to the Silicon Valley Report 2016, an estimated 443,000 people work in the Silicon Valley Innovation. Silicon Valley remains the global leader in innovation.

This is a real example of how supporting start-up entrepreneurs based on innovation and resilience can generate a major source of revenue for a nation's economy. Resilience is key to a successful business and, so it behoves on the government and the society at large to ensure that start-up entrepreneurs acquire the desired knowledge and support to enable them to become resilient in the ever changing economic and technological world of today "one who fears failure limits his activities. Failure is only the opportunity to more intelligently begin again" (Henry Ford, whose first two automobile companies failed)

Differentiation Strategy

Some may argue that entrepreneurs are born but entrepreneurs can also be made! We need to start teaching start-up entrepreneurs to have the mindset that

- Focuses on their means
- Set up an affordable loss
- Create partnerships – share risks
- Leverage surprises- how do they affect their means?
- Adaptive Execution-make small investments that will allow them to make bigger if upside is revealed
- Focus on what the can control rather than trying to predict
- Accept that setbacks and failure are likely but try to minimise their potential effects

(source: Professor Deniz Ucbasaran, An Entrepreneur's Journey Slides pp7)

This requires a plan of execution and therefore strategy is critical to the success of any business venture. As explained in the previous chapter, performance must be reviewed against targets. The whole business plan is a complete waste of time and resources if the plan of execution is not fit for purpose.

The plan of execution must detail who owns each milestone and the activities that would generate the required results. The various phases of the plan must be classified as 'projects' with outcomes.

This must be based on Porter's Five Forces Model and PESTLE. The Porters five forces includes the following

- The threat of new entrants to the industry
- The threat of substitute products
- The powers of buyers or customers
- The power of suppliers
- Rivalry among businesses in the industry

By determining the relative power of each of these forces, an organisation can identify how to position itself to take advantage of opportunities and overcome or circumvent threats. The strategy of an organisation can then be designed to exploit the competitive forces at work within an industry.

The dynamic nature of the competitive of the competitive environment means that the relative strength of the forces will change over time. Thus, it is important that the five forces analysis is repeated on a regular basis as to detect such changes before competitors and allow an early adjustment of strategy (David Campbell et al, Business Strategy Introduction pp 149)

The five forces regular analysis is very paramount to the success of the business as that serves as the catalyst to review performance. Milestones achieved should be measured using the information gathered from such analysis. Every change should be managed effectively to ensure that the business has a competitive advantage.

According to Porter (1985), competitive advantage arises from the selection of the general strategy that fits the business organisation competitive environment and then organising value adding activities to support the chosen strategy (David Campbell et al, Business Strategy pp195)

There are three main alternatives namely:

- Cost leadership
- Differentiation
- Focus

I would recommend 'differentiation' strategy as it is based on persuading customers that the product or service is superior to that offered by competitors. This relies on creating added value for the customer

Differentiation shall set the business apart from its competitors and always ahead of the strategy. A differentiation strategy is likely to necessitate emphasis on innovation, R&D, design and awareness of customer needs

Resilience

For an entrepreneur to turn around failure into a business, two related things must happen

- One must learn from failure
- One must bounce back and start again to apply what they have learnt

"I see a lot of people who want to do entrepreneurial things but who lack the resilience to see things through in tough times. I think this is one of the key attributes of a successful entrepreneur." (Nick Sanders, Head of Portfolio, Better Capital)

Resilience is very important for the entrepreneur to manage the affairs in times of uncertainty. When one have the tenacity, it will be proven in their strategic plan to make it happen. The global financial crisis of 2008 was not caused by subprime mortgages, credit default swaps, or failed economic policies but by a leadership failure. Entrepreneurs must be aggressive in the market place. Crisis often present an excellent opportunity to gain market share (Jeremy Kourdi, Business Strategy pp 149)

Resilience can be seen in a robust business plan but dependent on the strategy. According to the ideas of Kim and Mauborgne's Blue Ocean Strategy, an entrepreneur must answer the following questions:

- What is your winning aspirations?
- Why do you exist?
- What are you trying to achieve?
- If you can't win, then are you ready to play somewhere else?

From the Blue Ocean thinking, this can be expanded to include the following:

- A value proposition that attracts buyers: what is different about the offer? The value proposition must add value for customers to shift their focus onto the product or service being offered. If the product or service is just the same as others that are already on the market, then the business plan will not be fit for purpose and it will not be worth investing in such venture. There must be the reason why customers would buy a product, but most entrepreneurs start their businesses based on the hypothesis or assumptions
- A profit proposition that means the company makes money from the value proposition: As earlier pointed out, an entrepreneur must set out to make the business profitable. The value proposition must be the driver to maximise profits. In other words, the value added to service or the product introduced on the market must generate the required sales to guarantee profits. Any entrepreneur must have the mindset to maximise profits but that does not mean that one should expect to make profits at the early stage of the business. As a matter of fact, these strategic steps must give the entrepreneur the confidence to have the tenacity to pursue success.
- A people proposition that encourages the right behaviour from those within the company to deliver the strategy. This will impact how well the company executes? The behaviour of the people within the organisation must be shaped in accordance with the vision of the business This informs the capabilities that must be in place and it may require systems and measures that support the business capabilities

used to win in the chosen fashion and in the selected playing field (Richard Jones, Strategy Genius pp 233)

- Review of the performance must be carried out periodically to stay relevant and to ensure that any external factors causing changes are effectively managed. Change management is vital to ensuring that a business stays relevant and products or services tailored to meet the needs of the customer.

The crusade for a change must be started now to make the entrepreneurs of tomorrow ready and equipped to turn their ideas into systems that generate the revenue that is twice as much as the current revenue being generated from the small business sector. To do that, there must be the revolution to get the traditional business plan updated across board to include the strategic steps discussed in this research. Start-up entrepreneurs have also got to assess their background and private lifestyle as to whether they are ready to do all it takes to make their dream a reality. Sacrifice cannot be downplayed in the exploration of any business venture as it would demand time and investments to turn business ideas into business systems to create revenues.

The traditional system of using financial projections and accounts to fund businesses must be phased out as that does not augur well for successful start up to business. Using financial projections to decide whether a business is worthy for investment is absolutely outmoded and no longer sustainable.

"The assumption is that a firm is doing well if the key accounting number are moving in the right direction- increased sales, lower unit costs, higher productivity, enhanced margins, larger profits and so on. First, it is an inward-looking measure, with the result that seemingly good results can mask a worsening competitive position if at least some rivals are doing better" (Jules Goddard et al, Uncommon Sense, Common nonsense p27)

I believe strongly that numbers can be misleading as that does not give the true picture of who is running a business, whether the opportunity is really being maximised and above all it does not show the up to date performance of competitor

How much value does a business need to add for this to count as success. Performance is always relative-

Accelerating or decelerating, we need a standard of comparison. Traditionally, companies compare each year's performance with the previous year performance. Financial accounts are generally laid out. The assumption is that the firm is doing well if the key accounting numbers are moving in the right direction

A firm can justifiably be said to be winning if its share of wealth created by the strategic segment of which it is a member is growing faster than that of its rivals (Jules Goddard et al, Uncommon Sense, Common Nonsense)

I totally agree with this assertion that the financial performance or statement cannot be used as the sole document to assess the general of performance of the business in a specific industry. Although the key performance indicators might be good but that does not give the true picture of the performance of the competitors within the same industry and location.

Entrepreneurs must prove the viability of their business ideas by showing an in-depth analysis of the competition and a clear-cut strategy to outwit them and become the best out there. Such strategy must be owned by the entrepreneurs and must show a roadmap on how they will execute their plan and milestones to be achieved.

Just like individuals have personal development plan, every business must have an evolving plan showing how the business will develop based on assumptions and real potential risks as a result of its competition. A vision of how the business will be thriving in 5years and how it intends to get ahead of its competitors

Licensing or Certification for Start Up Entrepreneurs

A business plan without strategy is planning to fail. However, strategy is technical and cannot be self-taught. It must be taught within an environment to ensure that such skills transfer is validated, and the entrepreneurs certified or licensed to operate. This licensing procedure must not be bureaucratic but easy for start-up entrepreneurs to join with the main goal of getting the knowledge and skills for the ultimate success. This would prevent start-up entrepreneurs from ending up in unnecessary debts and for them to be resolute and resilient in their pursuit of success. This would also stop the waste of millions of pounds advanced as loans to these start-up businesses because many would think twice before making such a move as this study has proven.

The government will benefit as much as the start-up entrepreneurs when such licensing and training is implemented. It would minimise the high rate of business failure and save the government a lot of money. The entrepreneurs on the other hand would no longer be taken advantage of by any loan 'sharks' and would put them in a strong position for success.

Just as professional project managers are held in check by governing bodies, there is the need for a similar governing body for entrepreneurs in the country.

The main objective of such an organisation must be to support and review the progress of the execution of business plans. The entrepreneurs will be vetted against the strategic criteria discussed and this will separate the wheat from the chaff.

The failure rate will be minimised, and the turnover of business would increase astronomically.

Business strategy is never a once and for all event- it goes on and on. There is the need to continually review strategic objectives because the environment is always changing. Depending on the stance that a company adopts, the purpose of strategy is either to make a business 'fit' into its environment or to use the resources of the business to 'change the rules of the game'. By achieving this, the probability that the business will survive and prosper are enhanced (David Campbell et al, Introduction to Business Strategy pp 1).

The failures of these businesses discussed above could have been avoided if there was such a support system. From this study it is evident that the likes of Zirtual and Secret failed because of the lack of strategy and it is also evident from this research that these would-be entrepreneurs had no awareness of developing a robust strategy for the successful start-up of their businesses.

The ball is in the court of all governments and all interested stakeholders to help and support start-up entrepreneurs.

Chapter 9: Referencing

1. 2010-2015 UK Government Policy: Business Enterprise Report
2. The Telegraph May14th 2016
3. Theguardian.com
4. Mark Hurd, Chief Executive HP
5. Michel Syrett, Successful Strategy Execution
6. Sotirios et al, Strategy Practice
7. The Report on Small Firms 2010-2015
8. Half of UK Start Up fail within 5 years, Elizabeth Anderson
9. Companies House Report 2016
10. Jeremy Kourdi, Business Strategy
11. Steve and Spence 2008
12. Sara Carter et al, Enterprise and Small Business pp 112
13. Martin Ofori-Atta, How to Become a Successful Entrepreneur
14. http://uk.businessinsider.com/startups-that-failed-in-2015-2015-12?r=US&IR=T/#homejoy-2
15. WBS Entrepreneurship Module 2016, Exploring Business Opportunity Slides
16. Private Capital Management Slides 2015
17. David Gladstone et al, Venture Capital Handbook pp21
18. Christian Stadler, Enduring Success
19. Wikipedia, Five Forces Model
20. Richard A D Jones, Strategy Genius
21. Prof Diniz Ucbasaran, Entrepreneurship Module 2016
22. Mark McCormak, What They Don't Teach you at Harvard University
23. Thesun.co.uk (21/03/2017)
24. Wikipedia, Blockbuster LLC
25. Silicon Valley Report 2016
26. Henry Ford
27. David Campbell et al, Business Strategy
28. Nick Sanders, Head of Portfolio, Better Capital